To *Phyllis*

From

Rusty Anne

TREASURED FRIENDS

SHARING SPECIAL TIMES

Publications International, Ltd.

Louis Weber, CEO
Publications International, Ltd.
7373 North Cicero Avenue
Lincolnwood, Illinois 60712

Manufactured in China.

8 7 6 5 4 3 2 1

ISBN: 0-7853-2814-9

The inspirations in this book were written and compiled by Kelly Womer.

ONTENTS

FRIEND FOR ALL SEASONS

Friendship bears the fruits
of honesty, trust, goodness,
patience, compassion,
and understanding.
Friendship is always in season—
and always ripe to share
with others.

FRIEND FOR ALL SEASONS

A friend makes you feel like
you can do anything.
You can climb the highest
mountain, sail the widest ocean,
scale the tallest wall, and
realize the grandest dream.

FRIEND FOR ALL SEASONS

Friends are a little piece
of heaven on earth,
a treasure you can take with
you everywhere.

FRIEND FOR ALL SEASONS

In spring, a friend is the first daffodil
opening to greet the sunshine.
In summer, a friend is a black-eyed
Susan growing alongside a country road.
In fall, a friend is a chrysanthemum
giving thanks to the harvest moon.
In winter, a friend is a mistletoe
hanging above the doorway to share
peace and love.

FRIEND FOR ALL SEASONS

We are all travelers in
what John Bunyan calls the
wilderness of this world,
and the best that we find in our
travels is an honest friend.
He is a fortunate voyager who finds many.
We travel indeed to find them.
They are the end and the reward of life.
They keep us worthy of ourselves;
and when we are alone,
we are only nearer to the absent.

ROBERT LOUIS STEVENSON

FRIEND FOR ALL SEASONS

Two may walk together under the
same roof for many years,
yet never really meet; and two others
at first speech are old friends.

MARY CATHERWOOD

Friends have many things
in common.
But it's their differences that
make a friendship grow
and flourish.

Friendship is a place you can call
your own—where there's comfort in
knowing the door is always open
and the welcome mat is always out.

FRIEND FOR ALL SEASONS

Make new friends, but keep the old;
Those are silver, these are gold.
New-made friendships,
like new wine,
Age will mellow and refine.
Friendships that have stood the test—
Time and change—
are surely the best;
Brow may wrinkle, hair grow gray;
Friendship never knows decay.
For 'mid old friends, tried and true,
Once more we reach and youth renew,
But old friends, alas! may die;

FRIEND FOR ALL SEASONS

New friends must their place supply;
Cherish friendships in your breast —
New is good, but old is best;
Make new friends, but keep the old;
Those are silver, these are gold.

JOSEPH PARRY

FRIEND FOR ALL SEASONS

Build your friendship on the solid
foundation of loyalty and
trustworthiness, patience and
kindness, honesty and integrity.
Upon these solid principles, a
friendship will only grow stronger,
withstanding the winds of change
and storms of time.

FRIEND FOR ALL SEASONS

The secret of friendship is whispered
in the soft chirping of the first
robins of spring, the gurgling of a
creek in summertime, the wind
rustling the autumn leaves, and the
cool hush of a wintry day.

FRIEND FOR ALL SEASONS

Come walk with me
along life's path.
Come smell the fragrant
honeysuckle and fresh pine trees.
Come listen to the dove's soft coo
and the wolf's lonely howl.
Come taste the wild berries on
the vine and sweet sap
flowing from the maple trees.
Come feel the cool, morning dew
beneath your feet and the fuzzy
caterpillars inching along a branch.

FRIEND FOR ALL SEASONS

Come see the evening sun
disappear behind the hills and the
still lake reflecting the world.
Come walk with me.
And be my friend.

FRIEND FOR ALL SEASONS

FRIEND OF KINDNESS

To tell someone
"You are my best friend"
is the highest compliment
you could ever pay.
To be a <u>best</u> friend is the
highest honor.

and, you are.

FRIEND OF KINDNESS

The little girl stood all alone
on the playground.
The other children carefully jumped on
the hopscotch board drawn
in colored chalk on the sidewalk.
Some played hide-and-seek in
the nearby grove of trees
others scaled the monkey bars,
whizzed down the metal slide, and kicked
the soccer ball around the field.
There were screams of delight
and laughter.
But the little girl stood by herself, feeling
all alone in the midst of the commotion.
She was shy and couldn't imagine
asking the other girls if she could take a
turn jumping rope or playing a game.

FRIEND OF KINDNESS

Just then, another girl tapped her
on the shoulder.
"What are you doing?" she asked.
"I'm just watching," said the little girl,
trying to hide her interest in sharing
in the children's fun.
"Well, would you like to play on the
swing set with me?"
The little girl thought for a minute,
glancing at the empty and motionless
swings. They seemed lonely, too.
They seemed to need a friend. "Okay."
Together, they sat on the swings.
Together, they reached for the sky,
swinging higher and higher.
The little girl had never soared so high.
Sometimes, you never know where
friendship will take you.

FRIEND OF KINDNESS

We cannot tell the precise moment
when friendship is formed.
As in filling a vessel drop by drop.
there is at least a drop which
makes it run over;
so in a series of kindnesses
there is at last one which makes
the heart run over.

SAMUEL JOHNSON

FRIEND OF KINDNESS

FRIEND OF KINDNESS

A true friend safeguards you from
the burdens of the past,
the storms of today,
the uncertainties of tomorrow.

FRIEND OF KINDNESS

You hold a special place in my heart,
where our love will never depart.
Smiles of happiness meant to share,
a friendship filled with
kindness and care.

A little consideration goes a long
way in making a friend,
keeping a friend,
and being a friend.

FRIEND OF KINDNESS

Whenever you're sad,
you'll find happiness.
Whenever you're lonely,
you'll find good company.
Whenever you're tired,
you'll find rest.
Whenever you're questioning,
you'll find an answer.
Whatever you need,
you'll find it in a friend.

FRIEND OF KINDNESS

Friendship is the strong and habitual
inclination in two persons
to promote the good and happiness
of one another.

EUSTACE BUDGELL

FRIEND OF KINDNESS

Oh, the comfort, the inexpressible
comfort of feeling safe with a person;
having neither to weigh thoughts
nor measure words,
but to pour them all out, just as they are,
chaff and grain together,
knowing that a faithful hand will
take and sift them,
keep what is worth keeping,
and then, with the breath of kindness,
blow the rest away.

GEORGE ELIOT

FRIEND OF KINDNESS

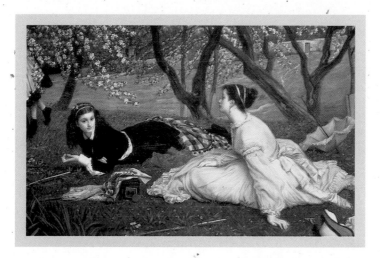

A friend is worthy of your trust and
deserving of your kindness,
for what you give to a friend
will be returned tenfold to you with
a heart of thankfulness
and gratitude.

FRIEND OF KINDNESS

It's safe to keep your feelings inside,
to never dare to be loved,
to never reach out in times of
sorrow and joy.
But to be safe is to miss the
comfort found in having a friend
and being a friend.

FRIEND OF KINDNESS

The only way to have a friend
is to be one.

RALPH WALDO EMERSON

Only when you are alone do you
fully realize the everlasting
joys of friendship.
It is in those solitary moments when
a friend seems to be at the heart
of your yearning.

FRIEND OF KINDNESS

FOREVER FRIEND

Distance doesn't separate the bond
between friends.
Friendship is simply the distance
between two hearts.

FOREVER FRIEND

You are my forever friend.
You accepted me just as I am but
also helped me realize all I could be.
You ignored my weaknesses and
praised my strengths.
You taught me how to
forgive and give.
You listened without judgment,
loved without any strings attached.
You laughed at my jokes,
and we laughed together until we
couldn't laugh anymore!

FOREVER FRIEND

You cried with me when clouds of
sadness rolled into my world.
You moved the clouds to
reveal a rainbow.
You walked with me through
a maze of decisions,
holding my hand around each
corner and guiding me toward the
right choice.
You trusted in me.
You showed me what being
a friend really means.
You are my forever friend.

FOREVER FRIEND

Friendship is a gift.
It's given from the heart,
wrapped in love,
accepted with gratitude,
and treasured forever.

FOREVER FRIEND

An acquaintance is someone who
knows you from the outside.
A true friend is someone who knows
you from the inside out.

FOREVER FRIEND

Growing up, we had slumber parties
on Friday nights and kept talking
even after the lights went out.
In school, you helped me with
my homework and helped me pick
out the perfect outfit for my first date.
Then we moved on to college,
careers, and families.
Our lives changed.
But our friendship remains
the same—as special as the sunny day
we first met on the playground.

FOREVER FRIEND

FOREVER FRIEND

A true friend cares in good
times and bad and
shares laughter and tears
when you're sad.
True joy is knowing a friend is
there with kind deeds and
smiles to share.

FOREVER FRIEND

Friendship is sewn with faith and
goodness, hope and harmony.
But only a single thread of love is
needed to hold two friends together.

Our friendship began the
day we first met.
It started with a handshake
and a smile.
It grew with kind deeds and
unspoken words.
It multiplied with unconditional
love and support.
Our friendship will never end.

FOREVER FRIEND

FOREVER FRIEND

The beauty of friendship is
never being afraid to be
yourself and always
knowing you'll be accepted
just the way you are.

FOREVER FRIEND

If you have one true friend you have
more than your share.

THOMAS FULLER

Hold a true friend with both
your hands.

NIGERIAN PROVERB

FOREVER FRIEND

FRIEND OF MANY BLESSINGS

Friendship grows a day at a time.
And each day, a new blessing
blossoms to be cherished for
many years to come.

FRIEND OF MANY BLESSINGS

A true friend is the greatest
of all blessings,
and that which we take the least
care of all to acquire.

FRANÇOIS LA ROCHEFOUCAULD

If you want to be inspired
If you want to be affirmed
If you want to be strengthened
If you want to be renewed
Then you must do no more than to
seek refuge in a friend.

FRIEND OF MANY BLESSINGS

May you always have

More smiles than frowns

More success than failure

More faith than doubt

More days than nights

More hope than sorrow

And more friends to make these

wishes come true.

FRIEND OF MANY BLESSINGS

You can count on me is the
unspoken promise from a friend.
The bond of friendship ensures the
words don't need to be uttered.

FRIEND OF MANY BLESSINGS

Show me a heart without
a best friend,
and I'll show you a life that
has yet to be touched by the gift
that comes from sharing
a beautiful part of yourself with
another human being.

FRIEND OF MANY BLESSINGS

A friend is like an angel who
has earned its wings but still
chooses to stay on Earth—
just to be near you,
guiding you in your ways, and
blessing your days.

FRIEND OF MANY BLESSINGS

Friendship always shines on
a cloudy day.
Sending rainbows to guide your way.
Bright colors of joy painted
with love.
A friend is a blessing from above.

FRIEND OF MANY BLESSINGS

You know you're a friend when . . .

. . . someone confides a secret in you

. . . someone comes to you first

to share the good news

. . . someone gives you a gift—

just because

. . . someone serves you with

a happy heart

. . . you're a friend in return.

FRIEND OF MANY BLESSINGS

A friend is a hand to help,
a heart to comfort,
a shoulder to lean on,
an ear to listen,
and an eye to behold
all your blessings from
head to toe.

FRIEND OF MANY BLESSINGS

Meeting a new friend isn't a
chance encounter.
It's the hand of divine intervention
that places two people in
the same place at the same time
to become one as friends.

FRIEND OF MANY BLESSINGS

The need to belong merely comes
from our being human.
It is the same with friendship.
We were born to achieve
such a great calling.

FRIEND OF MANY BLESSINGS

It is my joy in life to find
At every turning of the road
The strong arm of a comrade kind
To help me onward with my load.

And since I have no gold to give,
And love alone must make amends,
My only prayer is, while I live—
God make me worthy of
my friends.

FRANK DEMPSTER SHERMAN

Friendship is a single soul dwelling
in two bodies.

ARISTOTLE

We choose friends,
and friends choose us.
But friendship is more than
a decision.
It's a destiny that brings infinite
blessings and fills all our
days with meaning.

FRIEND OF MANY BLESSINGS

FRIEND OF BEAUTY

Begin a friendship with
a blank canvas.
Imagine the possibilities and
wonders waiting to be discovered.
Sketch your hopes and dreams.
Paint brushstrokes of colorful
moments and memories.
Frame it with unconditional
love and concern.
It will surely be a masterpiece
for all to admire.

FRIEND OF BEAUTY

Friendship is a symphony.
Each part must be played if there
is to be any melody.
Each member must stay in tempo
if there is to be any harmony.
Each note must be joined with
another if there is to be any music.

FRIEND OF BEAUTY

At each new chapter in your life,
reflect on the pages of
friendship that came before.
With them, a happy ending is
sure to follow.

FRIEND OF BEAUTY

Friendship is the highest degree of
perfection in society.

MICHEL EYQUEM DE MONTAIGNE

FRIEND OF BEAUTY

Think about the first time you
met your best friend.
Did you ever think you would share
the deepest places of your heart?
Did you ever imagine this would be
the first person you would turn to
for comfort and companionship?
Did you ever think you would
grow together as two souls
united in spirit?
The mystery and beauty of
friendship lie in the unending
journey of discovery.

FRIEND OF BEAUTY

Friendship can't be measured
in time.
It is measured in the many occasions
you were there to listen,
the many mornings spent chatting
over cups of coffee and tea,
the many afternoons spent
walking in the park,
the many evenings spent
gazing at the stars,
never having to say a word.
Friendship is timeless.
and a treasure beyond
measure

FRIEND OF BEAUTY

Every week, two little girls
celebrate a tea party.
One neatly sets the table and
"pours" the tea into the
empty teacups.
The other adds a cube of sugar
to stir in extra sweetness.
Together, they take a sip and smile.
Call it make-believe,
but their cups overflow with
friendship.

FRIEND OF BEAUTY

Take a walk in the woods and listen.
Do you hear the birds chirping?
Do you hear the squirrel scamper
through the trees?
Do you hear the water trickle
over the slippery stones?
Do you hear the wind calling
your name?
Nature is inviting you to
be its friend.

FRIEND OF BEAUTY

FRIEND OF BEAUTY

Blue is a cloudless sky.

Yellow is a field of sunflowers.

Red is a heart of love.

Orange is a setting sun.

Green is acres of towering trees.

These are the colors of friendship,

the colors of life.

FRIEND OF BEAUTY

Friends are necessary to a happy life.
When friendship deserts us we are as
lonely and helpless as a ship,
left by the tide high upon the shore.
When friendship returns to us,
it is as though the tide came back,
gave us buoyancy and freedom,
and opened to us the wide places
of the world.

HARRY EMERSON FOSDICK

FRIEND OF BEAUTY

Even when we don't talk, or I don't call, I know you are there and it is enough. When I call, those are the times that just knowing isn't enough.
your forever friend
Rusty Anne